"ON THE DESERT"
BY
DAVID L. EPPELE

Cover photo: Trichocereus huascha, a native of Chili, is a wonderful addition to any high-desert landscape. This plant bloomed 4 different times in one year! This morning, it insisted that I take its picture for the cover of On The Desert.   DLE

Artwork: Dal Clawson, Joseph Eppele, Mimi Kamp and El Jefe.

A special "thank you" to Leah Breasted, Janet Bocchino, Geneva M. Eppele, Ignacio Ibarra and Marvin Walker. They made this book a reality.

First Edition
Copyright 1990, Tortilla Press

Published and Distributed by:

TORTILLA PRESS
8 Mulberry Lane
Bisbee, Arizona 85603
USA
(602) 432-7040
ISBN 0-9622635-1-6

Printing by Ironwood Lithographers, Inc., Tempe, AZ

DEDICATED TO: THE DESERTS AND THEIR PEOPLES...

"Name one invention solely for the benefit of Mother Earth"

...David

INDEX

-prologue-
<u>Who in the heck is David L. Eppele and why does he have his own cactus garden?</u>

Arizona Cactus & Succulent Research really began when I was about nine years old. I was raised in Gallup, New Mexico, known as the "Indian Capitol Of The World." Some of my classmates were Navajo, Acoma and Zuni Indians. It was perhaps from them that I learned a different way of looking at nature.

"Grandpa can stare a hole right through my soul if he catches me stepping on plants he's trying to harvest," Art said. Melinda chimed in: "Mamma makes me sing a happy song to the Yucca plant before I can dig up sections of the root to make soap for our hair."

From this pretty savvy beginning I gravitated into the world of "ethnobotany" (a word that had not yet been invented) according to the fine principles of Dr. Edward F. Castetter, who headed up the Department of Biology at the University of New Mexico, in Albuquerque.

I became the note-taker. Scribbled like mad on a Big Chief nickel tablet all during the interviews with old Indians who were willing to share a bit of their plant knowledge with us. Later, Dr. Castetter (we lovingly called him Dr. Oso) would transfer these notes to his field journals.

Now Doc was good...darn good at finding out what uses the Indians had for just about any plant he would bring along for the interviews. He asked me to concentrate on the arid land plants, in particular the Cactus and Succulent families.

I'll skip a lot of neat years and neat stories, just to get on to Denis Cowper. I guess I hadn't been in Belen, New Mexico for two weeks when Denis picked me up hitching a ride along River Road. One look at his <u>extensive</u> cactus collection and it was all over. I was a confirmed 13-year-old cactus nut.

Well, Denis and I travelled all over the Southwest and down into Mexico collecting and mapping the distribution of Cacti, Agaves, Yuccas, Beargrass, Sotol....whatever struck our fancy. We passed on the data and many plants to Dr. Castetter, who was busy putting the data into what he called "first manuscript" form. He was preparing a book to be titled "<u>The Cacti of New Mexico</u>." Denis was an attorney...he spoke 7 languages, was educated in Europe (England and Germany) and had a mind like a steel trap! It was his idea that he and I form NEW MEXICO CACTUS RESEARCH. We published our findings world-wide. We set up branches in Japan, Germany, Great Britain and Australia. Life was a constant field trip!

Now here I am, nearly 40 years later, with Arizona Cactus & Succulent Research, Inc., a non-profit scientific and educational organization, doing the same things. Studying the plants of our deserts, preparing Dr. Castetters long awaited "Cacti of New Mexico," writing this self-syndicated newspaper column (which is the basis for this book) and delivering slide shows and lectures to just about anyone I can, talking about desert plants, ethnobotany, saving water, or perhaps simply reading some of my columns and answering "deserty" questions.

I'm also busy preparing a book on Indian uses of desert plants. I've added a few new wrinkles since Denis' unfortunate death a few years ago. Arizona Cactus has a seven-acre botanical garden right in our own back yard! There are well over 750 high-desert plants on display. Plants that will take the cold of the high deserts and can be used in a landscape setting.

We give free guided tours of the garden. Not just those little saunters through a place, but a tour with a live guide, someone who can and will answer your questions about the plants, birds, lizards and even the rocks. We'll laugh together with you over the antics of Flash, our "certified junk-yard dog."

Arizona Cactus is a membership organization. Our membership is scattered all over the world. We mail our monthly newsletter to 35 states and at least 5 foreign nations. Warning! The newsletter contains humor! And, we're "Spike's Cactus Club." because "Spike," Snoopy's brother who lives out on the desert, is an honorary member of Arizona Cactus.

With a membership organization, theoretically, the membership will build to a point where we won't have to sweat the modest bills we incur, but can concentrate on making the plant collection and the garden a true showplace and publish a ton of material through Arizona Cactus' publishing arm, Tortilla Press.

That's who Arizona Cactus is. Please come and see our garden! We're open from sunrise to sunset, seven days a week. Our address is: 8 Mulberry Lane, Bisbee, Arizona 85603. My title is "El Jefe De Las Plantas" or something. You can call me at (602) 432-7040. Early morning is best.

If, after reading "On The Desert" you are inclined to join Arizona Cactus in our efforts, please fill out the membership form cleverly tucked inside this book. (You'll never convince me you didn't see the form.)

Con Amor...

David

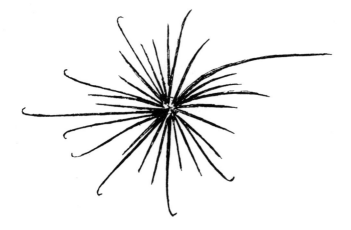

Another lousy day in paradise...

From the first day I saw Bisbee, Arizona I knew that I wanted to live in that town. I made up my mind that whenever I did move to Bisbee, I would quickly lock the door behind me!

Bisbee is one western border-town that somehow has escaped the crazy growth patterns of the 70's and 80's. You just aren't going to find a long avenue with nothing lining it but fast-food restaurants and auto repair shops. Bisbee almost got caught up in that scheme in the 50's with it's "dive-in" theater on Naco Highway.

Sure, there are a couple of "non-western-looking" buildings around, along with an abundance of restaurants, but somehow Bisbee has managed to escape the pitfalls of modern western urban sprawl.

Most newcomers who move to Bisbee want to do all they can to preserve the natural charm of Bisbee. They just don't want to see McDonald's Golden Arches cluttering up Main Street. One resident, who asked to remain anonymous, remarked: "If a franchise hits this town, it better be western in design, concept and operation!"

Bisbeeites can and should expect style restrictions on houses built on ridges and other prominent spots surrounding the city as expensive subdivisions crop up.

Bill Gillespie, former President of the Bisbee Chamber of Commerce said the question most frequently asked by both tourists and prospective newcomers is: "What about the crime rate?"

"What crime rate?" Bill responds with a laugh.

Then there's the climate...ah yes, the climate. Many people have asked me why I choose Bisbee as the home of Arizona Cactus & Succulent Research, Inc. "Because I can grow a greater variety of plants in Bisbee than anywhere else in the southwest," is my reply. The data to back up that statement can be found growing in our Botanical Garden, located 6 miles south of Bisbee.

I'm an early riser. As I look out my office window on any sunny day, I am met by the brilliant, proud morning, shining high over the desert. Something stands still in my soul. I am required to greet the day and I do so, in Navajo. "Yah Ta Hey!"

"How are you today, Brother sun?"

Same thing happens at night. I walk outside and look up at the thousands of stars visible with the naked eye around Bisbee. They fill the night air with a sense of fairness. "I'll twinkle for you...if you twinkle for me!"

Maybe that's the key to Bisbee. The modern visitors feel that stillness in their souls on arriving in Bisbee. In a heartbeat they fall in love with the town and the climate...they see the breathtaking light as we do.

A local pilot once told me someone called him on the plane radio while he was on final approach to the Bisbee Airport.

"What's the visibility around there?"

"Oh, about three days, I suppose," was our local pilot's reply.

Some western towns can be accused of being "all hat and no cattle."

Not Bisbee.

Artwork courtesy of the Copper Queen Hotel

Deserts are not easily defined

des-ert (dez′ert), n. (L. desertus, solitary, past part. of desertum, to forsake: de not + sertum to unite). 1. an unoccupied and uncultivated tract: a wilderness: a deserted region. 2. that which seems endless, barren, etc. (said of states of mind, periods of time, etc.) 3. a vast sandy or rocky expanse, almost destitute of moisture and vegetation. 4. an area devoid of positive character or quality: wasteland.

Do any of these definitions fit your mind's concept of a desert? Although the word desert is widely used, few stop to wonder exactly what the word "desert" means. To define desert is not an easy thing to do.

Strictly speaking, a desert is an area with an annual rainfall of 10 inches (25 centimeters) or less. The two largest deserts in the world are the Sahara in Africa and the great (sometimes called Gibson) desert of central and western Australia.

The world's largest desert areas lie between 20 and 30 degrees north and south of the equator in regions where mountains intercept the paths of the trade winds or where atmospheric conditions limit precipitation.

Deserts in the Southwestern part of the United States are called "deserts" for the most part because of the specially adapted plants and animals which inhabit those areas. For a purist in semantics (Dr. Hiakawa, USF, thank you), perhaps the only true desert region in the United States would be the very lowest regions of the Mojave Desert. Right there in the middle of Death Valley.

But it seems that over the years we have taken liberties with the word "desert" and included semi-desert areas of higher precipitation where moisture is lost by runoff or evaporation.

Remember that Hollywood concept of miles and miles of sand dunes, interspersed with an oasis every third day? Well, that's just about the closest thing to a real desert that the average person will see without jetting off to Australia or Africa.

Our little botanical garden here in Bisbee serves as a host garden for visitors from all over the world. The visitors from Africa and Australia are just amazed that we choose to call our part of the world a desert. "Why, it's so green!"...

"Embarrassingly lush."

Those are all references to our vast amounts of vegetation.

Long discussions with them result in their eventual admission that because our plant and animal life have truly adapted to these arid lands, we do, in fact, live on a desert...well, sort of.

Aussies and South Africans cling hard and fast to the purist definition of a desert. That is, their definitions describe a <u>climatic phenomenon.</u> When I point out that aridity can be due to other causes, such as extremely porous soils, they begin to bend...a little.

Then I slip in the fact that at high altitudes in polar regions, water may be present but frozen and not available for use. Haven't I just described a physiological desert?

Contrary to popular opinion, sand dunes cover only a minor portion of most deserts. Indeed, water rather than wind serves as the primary agent of erosion. The intense nature of desert storms, the lack of plant cover and the low absorptive capacity of the soil combine to cause rapid run-off and heavy erosion.

Since deserts are characterized by extreme temperature conditions, freezing can also act as an important erosion force.

While all deserts obviously share common features, each is different in its own way. Latitude, altitude, climate, physiography and other factors interact to make each desert physically unique and able to support a distinct assemblage of plant and animal life.

The four major deserts of the United States are, in order of age: The Chihuahua, The Great Basin, the Mojave and the Sonoran. Their boundaries shift with the winds.

On The Desert will take you on an armchair tour of the deserts. We'll introduce you to the peoples, plants, animals and ways of our deserts. Grab hold of that "remolino" (whirlwind) just over your shoulder and let's ride weekly...!

Some outrageous stories about Arizona

I have a 40-year file of stories about life in the Southwest. Newspaper clippings, magazine articles, books, letters and the cluttered mind, all sources for tales of our great land. These stories are filed and stored...ready for use. Many of these stories are termed "exaggerations." You know, those "Paul Bunyanish" yarns. The ones that stir the imagination.

How hot is it in Yuma?

"Well, back when they had the Fort there, a soldier died in his sleep, went to hell...and sent back for his blanket!

An Indian at Sasabe once told me: "the Javelinas down there (meaning Seri-land) ran around already cooked!"

Another "How hot is it?" story by Paul Dean, who was a columnist in Phoenix:

These folks were driving by car from Boston to San Diego. They stopped at a gas station in Gila Bend. The attendant was tanned to well-done and wrinkled like a prune. His eyes were faded and his hair looked just like strands of white straw. But boy, was he spry! He hopped around the car, cleaning bugs off the windshield. He checked the oil and water, kicked the tires and even cleaned the back window. (You know this story is a few years old!) Well, the city dude was indeed impressed. How could this shriveled-up old man be so spry and energetic in the 120-degree heat?

"This climate must really be good for your health," he said   to the attendant.

"Guess so," the fellow replied.

"Do you mind if I ask how old you are?"

"Nope," said the fellow..."Thirty-two."

Down here in Southeastern Arizona, the neighboring towns of Tombstone and St. David tend to contain citizenry who are definitely different from each other. Some of Tombstones finest citizens are known to take a drink; many of those in St. David are Mormons, who abstain. But the towns co-exist peacefully. Why, just last year a couple of St. David Mormons invited a fellow from Tombstone to go duck hunting with them early the next morning along the San Pedro. The Tombstone tippler and the two St. David warm-milk drinkers were in a duck blind along the river when a lone Mallard drake flew by.

BLAM!...BLAM! BLAM!...BLAM!..BLAM! BLAM!

6 shots filled the air with buckshot. The Mormons had both missed! The hombre from Tombstone stood shakily and let loose with one shot at the fleeing Mallard.

BLAM!

The duck fell dead, over a hundred yards away!

Then he turned, weaving and apologizing. "Usually, with a flock that big, I get at least four or five of the birds!"

Leroy Ballew, of Bisbee, tells this story about Mike Radonovich, a well-known rancher and steakhouse owner here in Southeast Arizona.

"Mike has a spread on the western side of Sulphur Springs Valley. Up kinda high, where the winds blow. And, he has a windmill up in a canyon, used to provide water for a stock pond. A young fellow moved in next door to Mikes place and put up another windmill. Mike jumped in his pickup and drove over by the windmill. The young man was standing nearby when Mike grabbed his 30-30 rifle from the rack inside the truck. He started firing rounds at the blades on the windmill! Well, this frightened the greenhorn so much he ran off. A couple of days later Mike gets a visit from a deputy sheriff.

"How come you scared that young fellow so badly?" asks the deputy.

"Looka here," says Mike. "It's hotter 'n hell around here.   There's no water. And then along comes this guy. He digs a well and throws up a big windmill, right in line with mine. Now dammit, you know there's not enough wind in this little canyon to run <u>two</u> windmills!"

Leroy says no charges were ever filed against Mike!

U.S. Forest Service:

<u>What has happened to Smokey Bear?</u>

A few weeks ago, I had a meeting with my Planning Committee concerning subject matter for "On The Desert." That "Committee" usually meets around 5:00 A.M. during summer time and perhaps a half-hour later during the winter months. Why so early? Well, some of us are night people and some are morning people. I'm a "morning person." I can get more work done between 5:00 and 7:00 A.M. than I can between 8:00 A.M. and 2:00 P.M. Less interruptions, cooler, mind is fresh...there are a lot of reasons.

The "Planning Committee" consists of Me, Myself and I. We have these long meetings devoted to various matters. Some mornings, the only decisions handed down are those involving the status of the coffee pot. Other mornings, ideas seem to jump from every corner of the mind.

I remember a couple of weeks ago, I was going to write an article on the dangers of forest fires. Now this takes some planning. Interviews must be arranged with National Forest supervisors. I set up these interviews and actually began putting the story together, when a rash of forest fires broke out. First in Mexico and then in the United States. The angle I was going to use was this: Whatever happened to "Smokey Bear?"

Most of you can easily remember all of the publicity that was generated by the U.S. Forest Service and Smokey.

<u>"Only You Can Prevent Forest Fires!"</u>

That was the big slogan. And it was very effective!

At least three generations of Americans were guided by the words of wisdom of Smokey.

Smokey was found near Capitan, (Ruidoso) New Mexico back in the 50's. He was himself the victim of a huge forest fire. He was drug from a smoldering mess of fallen trees, squalling just like any bear cub would be. The fire-fighter who found Smokey turned him over to a ranger of the Lincoln National Forest. Some bright person came up with the idea of using Smokey as a symbol of the seriousness of forest fires and a beautiful ad campaign was begun. One of the more successful "people motivating" campaigns ever undertaken by <u>any</u> government. It went on for well over 20 years. And then, nothing. Smokey seems to have been swept under the table! Guess he's hanging out with the "Roadrunner." Remember that great cartoon series?

In these days of "budget cuts," and restrictions on government spending, someone, someplace, has put " Smokey Bear" on a shelf. A whole new generation gives you a blank stare when you ask them about Smokey. Someone in the Forest Service or in the Department of Interior has their priorities messed up. Smokey worked in the 50's, 60's and 70's! With very little modification, Smokey Bear could very easily be teaching a whole new generation about forest fire prevention. No, not just forest fire prevention, <u>fire prevention!</u>

Wonder what it would take to bring back Smokey? Perhaps a coalition of the U.S. Forest Service and local fire districts. Sort of a pooling of advertising dollars.

There are some symbols that seem to work forever! Whatever it takes, let's bring back Smokey!

REMEMBER...ONLY <u>YOU</u> CAN PREVENT FOREST FIRES!

* Right after this column was published, I got a call from Elsie Cunningham, the Smokey Bear Program Manager. From her Washington, D.C. office, she told me about the new campaign the U.S. Forest Service was preparing. Said they were working with a Hollywood advertising agency to bring Smokey back into the limelight. First, one ripple on the pond. They sent out posters with color photos of flowers, animals, insects and fish. Smokey is right there at the bottom of the poster, reminding everyone that the forest is for every living thing, hoping each of us will be careful with our future. Good lines...great posters. So I've been waiting for the media blitz. I even watched Saturday morning cartoons to catch a glimpse of the new Smokey ads. Maybe I fell asleep? Oyes, Manny! Bring back Smokey, he'll know what to do!

Columns I didn't write this year...

I spent nearly two hours compiling an index of "On The Desert" columns published during the past year. When I printed it out, I couldn't help but think about all the columns I <u>didn't</u> write. Why, there were dozens of really neat ideas that the "Big Boss" shot down for one reason or another.

Well, I probably shouldn't be doing this, but the BIG BOSS is out of town this week, so I think I'll just use this space to let you, dear reader, know just what you've missed. Now don't go and say this is just another one of those columns full of "sour grapes" and whining and sniveling. This is a column designed to let you in on the "gate keeping" policies of certain "BIG BOSSES." Here, I will tell all...how ideas for column after column have been shot down for no good reason at all. How I have sweated and slaved over a hot IBM (trademark, registered, patented and sanctimonious) clone to bring you the most up-to-date information about our deserts. But does the BIG BOSS care? Why don't you be the judge? Let me dry my eyes and tell you just what those "meanies" have done to me over the past year!

I remember way back in January that I wanted to do another column on the Seri Indians and their habitat in Northern Sonora, Mexico. So, I asked for some advance travel money to go to Kino Bay for a couple of weeks to do some research.

"What you really want is a vacation in Kino Bay," growled the BIG BOSS.

Then, I wanted a column devoted to the new laser weapons, in relation to the removal of Bermuda Grass. The Department of Defense didn't even bother to call me back!

I contacted the BIG BOSS about a series of stories I wanted to write about desert landscaping in Las Vegas...and just because I wanted my expenses in advance, in quarters, that idea was squelched by "you know who."

Then there was the column on making wine out of the seed pods of Prickly Pear Cactus. We were just making a few "test batches" and I guess things got a little out of hand. But I don't think that was any reason for those editors to turn down my copy just because it was soggy and covered with splotches of red.

In June, I was willing to suffer through a week of meetings about the arid land plants of Australia...in Sydney...but again the BIG BOSS just hit the ceiling when Quantas called him to verify my tickets charged to his paper.

And then there was the column on off-road vehicles. I was going to write the owners side of the story, but the little Honda ATV just jumped right through the showroom window! I still maintain that they don't make plate glass like they used to!

Oh yeah, I almost forgot...in late August I called both Ford and Chevrolet, asking them to donate a 4-wheel drive crew-cab pickup to Arizona Cactus for use in our research. I'm still trying to find the phone number of someone called Helen Waite.

I was going to devote a whole column in September to desert gold mines. I had this great idea. Just get myself some good old weathered maps and a 750 pound magnet to pull behind my truck. The magnet is still firmly attached to a cattle guard over by Quartzite, Arizona. Old sour puss just about had a fit when I turned in the bill for that!

Helicopter time up on the great Basin Desert seemed like a reasonable request of the Bureau of Land Management. I can still hear their screaming laughter!

In October I heard that this Italian firm was going to unveil a brand new desert vehicle capable of awesome speeds on the desert floor. Do any of you know someone named Helena Esperanzi?

I was going to write about the paint companies and those names they come up with for colors of paint...like "Desert Pom Pon." "Really Red Rising Sun" and "Quiche Sans Sand." Neither their public relations folks or anyone in management returned my calls.

Now rumors are floating around the newsroom. I heard them as I was turning in this column. Seems the BIG BOSS is negotiating to buy a newspaper out on the Gobi Desert. Furthermore, it seems that I'm being considered for a "special correspondent" assignment, maybe permanently!

Alright! Wow!

"Intense Gardening" ways of the ancient ones

Pick up nearly any copy of "Organic Gardening" and somewhere in between all the advertising copy you'll find references to a gardening technique called "intense gardening." Intense gardening is nothing new. It has been practiced by arid land gardeners on all continents for thousands of years.

Intense gardening basically means that you will grow all the fresh vegetables you and your family need for a year in a 400 square foot space (that's a 20' X 20" plot). I know it sounds impossible, but it has worked for Chinese gardeners long before John Deere invented a green grasshopper and called it a tractor. That's not a "put down" of John Deere products. Knowledgeable farmers world-wide smile and feel a warm glow when they are asked: "How long does a John Deere last?"

Organic Gardening (I have a friend who has re-named that magazine "Orgasmic Gardening") alternately credits the French and the Chinese with the introduction of intense gardening techniques. Then there were the Egyptian gardens along the Nile. Don't forget the wonderful gardens along the confluence of the Tigris and the Euphrates.

Here in the Western United States, all agriculturally-oriented Indian tribes practiced their versions of "intense gardening." They dug up a small plot of land. Then they removed all of that freshly dug soil to a depth of 6 inches. It was stacked up along the outer perimeter of the plot. Then they went back in the plot and turned another 6 inches of soil. Then the Indians threw small bones, dried leaves and twigs on top of the soil and then added about one-third of the outer soil on top of this. The remaining soil was then banked around the perimeter of the plot to form a natural barrier...to keep rain water (or irrigation water) in. Old Indians at the Jemez Pueblo in New Mexico told us they caught fish by hand and net in the Jemez River. They cut the fish into small pieces and used them for fertilizer.

"makes the earth breathe," was the best quote we got when we asked foolish questions regarding mulch.

The editors at Organic Gardening have coined the phrase "double digging" for this method of soil preparation. I"m positive the Indians we interviewed never used those words!

Back to the plot: Plant tall crops (i.e. corn) around the outer edge of the garden. Sow these seeds <u>very</u> close, about an inch deep. Now, gather up all of the seed of those veggies you really like. Mix them all together and scatter that seed inside the garden plot. Then import at least a half-inch of good topsoil (I use the soil under Mesquite trees) to cover the seed. Smooth the soil over the seed, lightly tamp it down and slowly flood the plot with water.

By now you realize you haven't followed the instructions correctly....you used the soil piled up around the perimeter of the plot and water is running everywhere. Now, go get some soil and build another dam around the plot. Tamp that soil tightly, so that water remains inside the garden space.

When all the seeds sprout, you'll have a great time trying to tell a bean plant from a watermelon. Go and talk to someone named Jack. If, after two months, you still can't tell one plant from another, go to your seed store and stare at the seed packages for an hour or so. At least you know the corn is that tall stuff shading the other plants from the sun and harsh dry winds.

That's all there is to it: double dig the plot, leaving a basin to catch the water, mulch the soil and use lots of seed. A natural crop rotation takes place as the early-bearing vegetables are harvested, leaving room for the giant Ninja Mutant Teenage Squash to take over the plot for the fall!

Since the Indians were growing wild plants native to their regions, these plants were adapted to the climate and soils. These plants certainly didn't need much coddling. Summer rains took care of the watering requirements.

Mint, sage and oregano plants grew right in with the giant white Lima bean plants. Tomatillos have no problem seeking and maintaining their own growing space, usually right beside the chili tepin. Onions grew right next to the potatoes so the gardener could occasionally trim the onion plant, making the eyes of the potato water, providing ample moisture for the other veggies!

Seriously now, weeds would fight for some space to grow, but they are smothered out by the vegetables.

One old Indian at Zia Pueblo told me the best garden he raised in over 79 years was one that he planted in the first week of June!

"I broke my leg that spring and couldn't prepare my family plot. Others offered to do the work for me, but I did not allow that. Something told me to wait...that things would work out. By June, I crawled on my knees to the garden site and began preparing the earth. Since I was so close to my work I took extra time in mixing the soil. By crawling around the outer edge, I had the earth packed firmly. In August, a big rain flooded many of the tribal gardens and washed them out. Mine was packed so tightly that it held nearly 6 inches of rainwater! Big Crop! Plants grew when they were supposed to...they didn't have to struggle through the cold spring months."

If you want to try this gardening technique, you'll also probably want to plant some native seeds. Hardly a week goes by that my mailbag doesn't have a letter from a reader wanting to know a source for native seeds. Here's my list of reliable sources:

Plants Of The Southwest
1812 Second Street
Santa Fe, NM 87501   (Send $1.50 for a super catalog)

Desert Moon Nursery
P.O. Box 600
Veguita, New Mexico 87062 (catalog $1.00)

Native Seeds/SEARCH
Tucson Botanical Gardens
2150 N. Alvernon Way
Tucson, Arizona 85712 (catalog $1.00)

Talavaya Seeds
P.O. Box 707
Santa Cruz Station
Santa Cruz, New Mexico 87567

Summer care of cacti and succulents

Most cactus and succulent plants reach their growing peak in late June and early July. That's the time to do some pruning. If you prune your plants at this time, the job will be much easier than if you wait until the middle or latter part of the summer. In fact, pruning desert plants during the monsoon season is really not a good idea. The freshly cut ends of the plants will absorb moisture and set up a rot condition. This will eventually kill the plants.

Most of our calls about plant care during the summer months are about the trimming of Prickly Pear cactus. The calls go something like this: "I would like to donate some cactus plants to Arizona Cactus' botanical garden."

"What kind of cactus plants?" I ask.

"Oh, some Prickly Pear and something that looks like a candelabra, I think it's called a Cholla. We have lots of them and you're most certainly welcome to take all you want."

Then, I mention that we charge for landscape services such as the cleanup of their cactus patch and the caller either hangs up, or simply cannot understand how we could turn down the offer of free cactus plants!

Here's how to trim those unruly plants. You'll need a pair of leather gloves, a sharp butcher knife and a large pair of kitchen tongs.

Begin with the outer pads, those hanging over into your neighbors yard. Grasp the pad with the tongs and cut the pad at the base, where it is connected to the mother plant. A word of warning here: Be sure and grasp the pad that you want to trim towards the middle. Get the balance of the pad, because when you make your cut, the pad will be heavy! (They contain a great deal of liquid) Make a clean slice. You'll discover that this is really easy to do...much like cutting into a melon. There, that was easy...now on to the next one. Now, don't get crazy and get in a hurry with this job! You may wind up wearing the pads!

Many cactus growers sprinkle flowers of sulfur on the exposed freshly cut surface of the parent plant and on the cut surface of the pad you've just removed. This prevents an infectious rot condition from getting started and also drives all the little creepy-crawlies crazy! Flowers of sulfur should be available in bulk at your local plant nursery. Place the pads you want to transplant in the shade for a few days. This allows the plant to form a protective crust over the cut area. Now plant the pads with the cut portion about two or three inches deep in half sand and half soil. <u>Do not water the plant!</u> During the summer months, it takes only a couple of weeks for the plant to send out a whole new root system. It will do this in dry soil. Trust me. Let's suppose you've planted a prickly pear pad a couple of weeks ago. Go out and lift the pad out of the soil with your tongs. If you see the new little roots sprouting, carefully bury the pad back in the soil at it's original depth. Now you may water the plant. Remember, if you water the plant before it has a chance to send out new roots, it can, and will rot. You see, the culture of cacti is exactly 180 degrees different than the culture of leafy plants.

The Succulents of the desert lands, the Agave, Ocotillo, Beargrass, Sotol and Yucca, require moist soil to survive transplantation. Make individual wells for these plants and keep them moist while they are sending out new roots. <u>Never make wells for your cactus plants!</u> They just hate to get their feet wet!

If you wish to transplant cactus plants that have a full root system, do so during the spring or summer months and give them a big drink of water immediately. Don't drown the poor things...it has often been said that the biggest enemy of a cactus plant is someone with a garden hose.

You can trim your cholla cactus the same way as prickly pears. Remember, each joint of a cholla, or prickly pear cactus is a potential new plant.

When you trim your cacti...take your time. Don't make any sudden moves around them. Keep your mind on the job at hand. A pad of prickly pear can fall on your foot and just ruin your whole day.

To trim really large cactus plants, I use a flat shovel. I sharpen the back edge of the shovel with a flat file, or on an electric grind-stone. It then becomes my knife. One can easily cut the pads with the sharp shovel, then slip the shovel under the middle of the plant and pick up several of the pads at once.

Many varieties of prickly pear cactus have pads with hundreds, no, make that thousands, of tiny small spines. If one of these pads falls on your arm, or another part of your body, you're in trouble! Here's an easy way to get rid of those tiny spines. Get some white glue...Elmer's glue comes to mind. Carefully spread a thick layer of this glue on the afflicted part of your bod. Now let it dry...thoroughly. This

15

may take up to 10 minutes. When it is completely dry, peel the glue off. 95% of the spines will be removed along with the layer of glue.

When transplanting fully-rooted cactus plants, here's a trick I learned back when I was an Indian...I usually pre-dig the holes where I want the plants to call home. Then I carry the freshly dug up plant to the hole, set it in and begin filling in the hole with the dry dirt I removed while digging the hole. I get a stick, or some tool to hold the plant upright while I fill in the hole. Then I pack the dirt tightly around the plant. Use the handle of the shovel to assist you. Give the plant a good drink of water and your job is over. Since cactus plants store water for use during dry spells, you really don't have to water more than once a week during the summer months. If you should miss a week or three, don't worry about it. Rest assured, the plant will survive.

Cacti do not require exotic soil mixtures to survive. In fact, most of those soil additives harm the cacti by retaining moisture, inviting an unscheduled visit from Mr. Rot. Half sand, half soil...that's all there is to it. Plant food? I sprinkle a little systemic rose food around my plants once or twice during the summer. And I still haven't used up a 20 pound sack I bought 2 years ago.

One last thing: Cacti do sunburn! When you remove a plant, make a note of the south side of the plant. Mark it with something...stick a piece of paper or cloth on the spines. When you plant your cactus, make sure your marker is facing south.

Good growing!

Winterizing your desert garden

There are certain chores that need to be completed before the first big frost of the year settles upon the desert. Drain, clean and cover the swamp cooler. Did you shut the water supply line off? Cover your outside water faucets. Drain all garden hoses and store them and don't forget to cover your frost sensitive plants. I use black plastic to cover the frost sensitive plants on display in our garden here at Bisbee Junction. I cut pieces of 4 or 6 mil black plastic large enough to completely cover the plant and tie it with string. If the plant is a tall one, I tie it in several places. You'll need to make a bow knot that you can easily untie next spring. One year I got kinda crazy and tied the plants with a series of heretofore unheard-of knots. They got wet during the winter and the twine shrunk, resulting in knots that no one could untie!

What happens to a cactus plant covered with black plastic during the winter months? Nothing! These plants are normally dormant during the winter months. They rely entirely upon moisture stored inside themselves during this period. Their plumbing system is shut down to prevent freezing.

Which plants should you cover? Cover those plants that are not native to your deserts. Just about all cacti will survive a winter on the low deserts, but once you get off the desert floor, many of the plants are in danger of being nipped by Jack Frost. Just what does a frozen cactus look like? Black...the plant turns black, or grayish black.

DO NOT COVER YOUR CACTUS WITH CLEAR PLASTIC!

The plants will sunburn if you do that. What does a sunburned cactus plant look like? It turns yellow.

I do not water any of the plants on display here in our garden during the winter months. These plants survive entirely on the moisture stored inside them. Remember, the culture of cactus plants is exactly opposite of other plants.

Don't try to transplant cactus plants during the winter months. They will not re-root or re-establish themselves and they will die. The tiny root systems will freeze. Remember, these plants are dormant at that time of year. You may transplant other desert succulents in the winter. Agaves, Ocotillos, Beargrass, Sotol and Yuccas may all be transplanted during the cold months. However, when you transplant them to their new home, don't over-water them. Give them just enough to firm up the soil around the base of the plant. Begin watering them in the springtime.

Many cactus plants turn purple during the winter months. That's normal. It's just their way of saying: "Wow! It's really cold out here!"

Many of the cactus plants produce a chemical much like the one that makes beets red, or purple. By producing that chemical, they can absorb more heat and survive the cold weather. Remember, light colors reflect heat while darker colors absorb heat.

The more I study the plants in the cactus family, the more I come to believe that these plants wrote the book on SURVIVAL!

The secret life of plants...watch out! (your plants may be listening)

During the past ten years, there has been a great deal of publicity related to the ability of plants to respond to various stimuli. Remember reading that plants respond to music? Play some stringy "mood music" and your plants will respond with increased growth. One of our members sent us a book for our research library that is truly amazing. The title is "The Secret Life of Plants," by Peter Tompkins and Christopher Bird. In one sentence, the book is a fascinating account of the physical, emotional and spiritual relations between plants and man.

Here, in one mind-boggling volume, the authors have digested a vast amount of material pertaining to the mysterious inner-life of plants and how this life affects (and is affected by) the animal kingdom, particularly man.

Despite the "out of this world" flavor of the book, it is not science-fiction, but a serious compilation by two well established scientific researchers. Peter Tompkins is well known for his book "Secrets Of The Great Pyramid." Christopher Bird is a biologist and anthropologist of note. The theme and tenor of the book rests on the philosophy that all living things (and some presumed non-living) are inter-related. In other words, what affects one, affects them all.

Among the more bizarre statements advanced by the authors relate to plants that "count" and plants that "talk" and even plants that show signs of being in "heat."

Mrs. Harold Hashimoto, the wife of a Japanese Doctor of Philosophy and a successful electronics engineer, was able to get a cactus (genus not stated) to respond to her assurance that she loves it. When this "response" was transformed and amplified by her husband's electronic equipment, it produced a high-pitched hum with a decidedly varied rhythm and tone, much like a song! In fact, the good doctor said the song seemed at times, to be "warm and jolly!" In time, the Hashimotos became so intimate (sic) with their plant they were able to teach it to count and add up to twenty. In answer to a query as to how much two and two are, the plant would respond with sounds which, when transcribed back into inked tracings, produced four distinct and conjoined peaks!

Another incredible attribute of plants is the seeming ability to transmute, in alchemical fashion, phosphorous into sulfur, calcium into phosphorus, magnesium into calcium, carbonic acid into magnesium and nitrogen into potassium. But nowhere does the book state that the plants can change lead into gold.

In 1963, Pierre Baranger, a professor and director of the laboratory of organic chemistry at the famous Ecole Polytechnique in Paris, France, incontestably proved that in the germination of leguminous seeds in a manganese-salt solution, the manganese disappeared and iron appeared in its place.

Then finally, there is a chapter of the book which deals with the radionical treatment of plants. The plants were cleared of insect infestations not directly, but by treating a photograph of the area!

The authors have documented their statements with some 18 pages of bibliography. No lover of nature or searcher of truth dares to leave this book unread!

Excuse me now, I'm going out to the greenhouse to switch on some vintage Brubeck jazz for my plants...they demand it...and certainly deserve it!

Designs on the desert floor

One of the unsolved mysteries of modern archaeology is preserved on the desert up on a mesa which is part of the Big Maria Mountains north of Blythe, California. It is also part of the National Register of Historic places.

Scientifically, they bear the name anthropomorphic geoglyphs. They are called "intaglios" by the people living around Blythe. An intaglio is a design or figure incised beneath the surface of hard metal or stone.

Most of these designs were made by scraping the darkened surface rock on the desert floor to reveal a tan-colored soil beneath. This lime-based soil has weathered thousands of years of rain, scorching desert sun and heat and the westerly winds of the area.

The figures were fashioned by Indians possibly thousands of years ago, but their cultural significance is uncertain. Various Indians such as the Mojaves, Yumas, Halchidomas, Quechans and Maricopas inhabited the area, but no concrete evidence linking the figures to any particular group has been discovered, even after recent investigations by archaeologists from the National Register and the Native American Heritage Commission.

A variety of theories surround the origin and significance of these giant desert figures, which are best seen from the air. George Palmer, a pilot from Blythe, first discovered the giant desert figures while flying over the area in 1930.

He reported seeing "giant horse tracks" leading from the Colorado River to the base of the mountains where the figures are located. The sites are generally found along the Colorado River flood plain; however, they are also found in San Bernadino and Imperial Counties. The specific locations are not identified in order to discourage vandalism.

That problem arose some 20 years ago and it was only recently that the Bureau of Land Management erected chain-link fences around three of the major figures north of Blythe.

This is part of the Bureau's new image, that of protector of the lands. A welcome change after many years of questionable stewardship.

Where did these giant figures come from?. What is their significance?

One author uses the giant figures, which he claims are found nowhere else on the continent, as evidence for his theory that primitive man was at one time visited by highly intelligent beings from outer space.

Eric Von Daniken, in his book "Chariots Of The Gods," theorized that man was visited while the planet was relatively young and our ancestors were in their primitive stages.

He claims that these giant desert figures can only be seen from the air where the original calculations were made and given to the Indians below who followed the instructions in carving out the figures. Most of the carvings are from six to eight inches deep.

He added that the figures can also be seen from the ground, but only make sense when viewed from the air and were, possibly, some sort of landing guide for the extra-terrestrial visitors.

Well, that's one claim. Another is that one of the Indian tribes had a da Vinci in their midst, who went around creating "big art!"

I do know this much: Von Daniken's claim that these figures are found only around Blythe are simply not true. Some years ago, I was part of a plant survey team that flew over large parts of southeastern Arizona, southwestern New Mexico and northern Chihuahua, Mexico. There are geoglyphs around Tucson's airport, some near Casas Grandes, Chihuahua, Mexico and others around Silver City, New Mexico. These sites do not have figures a quarter of a mile long as the one at Blythe, but they are large. There is also a site reported near Nazca, Peru.

Perhaps a closer study of the trading routes set up by early Indian tribes in the United States and Mexico will lead us to a simpler answer to one of the many mysteries now found "On The Desert."

A Grand Canyon sunrise

In the morning, just as dawn spreads a soft glow of light throughout the room, I crawl out of my sleeping bag, pull on my pants, then my boots, grab a cotton shirt from the sofa and quietly head towards the door. A little voice inside says..."turn the porcelain doorknob slowly, so the squeak won't wake the others. Slooowly....! There, that's it! Now, gently pick up on the door, or it will drag against the flagstone floor." But, when I did that, the top hinge squalled like a cat at mealtime!

I step out onto the porch and a blast of cool, almost frigid air covers my face and chest. I shiver as I put on my shirt. The light is growing brighter and I'm missing at least a thousand pictures with each minute that passes!

I reach back and carefully close the door behind me. It scrapes against the flagstone and I think the whole house will fall down! You see, I'm an active nine-year-old and doing things that slowly seem like living in the slow motion picture world of the "Chief" movie theater in Gallup, New Mexico...my home town.

"Click," goes the lock. Now I'm free! I've done it! No one was awakened during my early morning attempt to be the first person to greet the rising sun! I turn and take five giant steps towards the iron pipe handrail surrounding the rock porch. My hand brushes the cold black pipe. I stop and begin buttoning my shirt. I look out over the rock spires and begin counting the plateaus from the bottom up. Eight...nine...ten! Yep, they're all still there...and every rock is just where I left it last night! Uncle Charlie says each level represents a different water level of some year gone by. Well, if I'm standing here on 1945, then down there, halfway down the Grand Canyon, must be 1920, I figure...or maybe 1910? Aw, forget it!

I jump down the tan rock steps, taking them five at a whack, just like the paratroopers. I spin around the first landing and jump the next ten steps, this time I figure I'll jump six on the first leap and then four the second. "Plop." I hit the long ramp leading to the very edge of the world on a dead run. "Smack." right up against the lower guardrail. I grab the rail, duck my head and swing myself out over the edge of the landing, throwing my legs out as far as I can. Why, Superman himself would have a hard time doing that! Holding the rail tightly, I pull myself back and sit on the flagstone landing. I think to myself..."This is sorta like early morning mass...looking at the sheer vastness of this canyon...only better!"

There, over to the east, is the rising sun. Red at first, just peeking over the edge of the world. I glance down at the shadow caused by my leg. I reach for a rock, to scrape a mark that identifies a reference point I'll use later. Sort of a testimonial to the swiftness of the sunrise.

Looking up towards the west, a splash of sunlight covers the top edge of some far off side canyon. Quick, look back to the east! You're missing the action! There, the sun is nearly a quarter of the way out of the earth's belly and now it's almost orange. " Same color as orange soda pop," I quip. Off to the right, a clump of cactus, sitting out alone on the edge of a rock cliff, catches my eye. "Why the red flowers are open! Did they stay that way all night? What causes that?"

I look down at my reference point...and...it's gone! "No, dummy, you looked at the black edge of the shadow." There, back almost an inch, maybe more, is the chalky line you drew just minutes ago...but...it seems as if an hour as passed." My mind asks, "Can we ever make time stand still?"

One thing for sure...The Grand Canyon can!

Dining on the desert...the 200 mile wine

The native plants of our American deserts have been a source of food for man "since our cousins, the Comanches, left the mountains and went out on the plains," said Manuel.

We were visiting the Indian Pueblo at Taos, New Mexico. The big question of the day seemed to be: "What do you eat in times of crop failure or when you're down on the deserts?"

For some strange reason, we wound up with two Indian informants sitting beside us. Most of our interviews were conducted with a single informant, but this beautiful spring morning found Dr. Castetter (Dr. Oso) and me talking to a couple of seemingly ageless Taos residents.

Now, these two old men were just not the average informants. Antonio and Manuel were the "town clowns." A lady in Santa Fe warned us..."those two make us pull our hair! With all of their antics they should have been taken away with the circus long ago! They're two tricky coyotes, so be careful how you phrase your questions!"

Our backs were being warmed by the adobe wall that had been absorbing the sun blazing away in the east-southeast sky. I was shading my eyes, watching a hawk circle the Pueblo, when Dr. Oso nudged my elbow and threw me one of those "better get this down!" looks.

I began scribbling...as Manuel said:

"I remember telling you that I went to the Mission School around 1886. I was just 17 years old and felt very uncomfortable at the school over in Taos. My place seemed to be in the fields and forests, not in this white man's school! Antonio here felt the same way. Why, we ran away almost every week! We ran off to a special cave just east of here and talked about the Old People. We were always interested in what They thought and did. They often told of the fights they had with the Cheyennes...the Pakanbos."

"What does that word mean?" I thought...

"That means "fight like dogs," said Dr. Oso...for my benefit.

I laughed to myself as I continued writing...

"In 1854, my father went to hunt deer in the mountains east of the place you call Folsom. It was late spring and the snow still covered our Sacred mountain.. The whole tribe had just survived a very hard winter and were badly in need of meat for the Pueblo. He and his party crossed the Rio Colorado (Canadian River) near the part where the river makes a big slow turn back to the east. When they got out onto the grasslands, the Cheyennes attacked them. They fought for three days and lost half of their hunting party. My father said he and two others ran south down onto the high deserts east of a place called Estancia. Since they were on the run they lived off the young flower stalks of the Yuccas they began encountering. If their eyes spotted a flower stalk above the plant, they passed it by. They were looking at the plant tops, trying to see the new green color, which meant it was "giving birth." When they spotted one such as this, they would chop out that new growth with their stone axes they carried with them. This life-giving tool was a hatchet-head shaped stone, tied to a cedar or oak handle with the fibers of the Yucca plant. This young flower stalk provided them with a sugary fibrous mush they made into little trail cakes. They always said a prayer before chopping up the stalk because it was "not right to kill the newly born of this plant."

Antonio: "But this was a life or death situation which provided them with an exception to the rules!"

Manuel passed up this chance to argue with his old friend and continued: "They saw the sickly newly planted corn fields of the Spaniards and raided them, committing an even bigger sin...they pulled up the young corn stalks and ate them. But they only pulled up every other stalk, so the Spaniards would not notice plants missing in the rows. I can still hear my father laugh as he described those crazy rows of corn the Spaniards planted. He could never understand why they didn't plant corn the way that he did!"

Antonio picked up the story here:

"After six days of running, they arrived back here at the Pueblo. They went to the Governor to tell him what had happened on their trip. Others from the party were entering the Pueblo from different directions. Some were packing meat! But many told of the death left behind. The Governor was very sad, but he praised the men for their valor and accepted a sack of the trail cakes from Manuel's father. These trail cakes were beginning to ferment! All of the tribal leaders went and made

26

wine from the cakes and stayed drunk for two full days! Why even today, the fine Yucca wine we make is still called the 200- mile wine!

Tumbleweed salad...a gourmet delight?

The desert West has one plant that we may well have been able to live without. The Hopi Indians call the plant "White Man's Plant." It's an introduced plant from Eurasia called Russian Thistle. Better known in the West as tumbleweed. Songs have been written about the plant, a well-known newspaper cartoon series bears that name and it's one of the primary sources of hay fever...ranking right up there with ragweed and bermuda grass.

The botanical name of the plant is <u>Salsala kalis</u> and our variety is known as tenufolia. There's another variety in the midwest known as collina. A nicer name and a nicer plant. By the way, "kali" is an Arabic name meaning fierce, or sharp. The genus name is from the Latin, "salsus," meaning salty, referring to the plants' liking for alkaline soils.

The plant was introduced to the American deserts in hopes it could be used as a forage crop and soil stabilizer. Guess things got out of hand, because the plant seems to grow better than any other desert plant and certainly with much less water. Farmers and ranchers have learned to make livestock food from tumbleweeds, both as hay and in pellet form.

Some cottage industries have figured out how to compact the large dried plants into logs, called "tumblelogs." They sell them as fuel for your wood stove and fireplace.

In Southern Europe (Spain and Portugal), the ashes of tumbleweed were once used in the production of an impure carbonate of soda called "Barilla."

I can remember the first time I saw a tumbleweed, a <u>big</u> tumbleweed, rolling along the railroad tracks in front of a train. Here was this huge locomotive, pulling a freight train along at 50 miles an hour. The engine's whistle was being blown for a railroad crossing. I didn't see the crossing, so I thought it strange the engineer would be blowing the whistle for the tumbleweed to get out of the way! I also remember rooting for the tumbleweed to win the race!

Desert travellers have been known to have serious auto accidents when a big brown ball, three or four feet in diameter, crossed the highway in front of their car. Many motorists feel they must swerve to get out of the way, or worse yet, come to a complete stop in the middle of the highway to let the tumbleweed have the right of way. Now, that can get messy! I have seen a couple of rear-end collisions caused by tumbleweeds. In both accidents, there was serious personal injury. That big weed won't hurt your little old car! It may leave insignificant scratches on the paint job, but those are easily rubbed out. There's a pun there, but I'll leave it alone.

Tumbleweed first found its way into the United States mixed in with Russian flax seed. The seed was brought into South Dakota in 1873 and by 1898, Russian thistle was established down in Colorado. It was introduced along railroad tracks throughout the west by falling out of grain cars. Russian thistle is not a true thistle, but rather a member of the Chenopodiaceae or goosefoot family. Other members of that family include lamb's quarters, cultivated beets and spinach.

Gardeners know they're in trouble when thousands of little tumbleweed plants sprout overnight and seemingly carpet the garden plot. The only consolation is that they are easily removed in the first three or four days. But if you're like me, you'll put off weeding for just a few more days and wind up with a real first-class weeding job on your hands.

Now, if the tumbleweeds are under three inches tall, try making a salad with them. That's right...salad! They are tender and succulent at this stage, but grow rapidly and soon become tough. After you gather up a sackful of the small shoots, rinse and trim the roots from them. The young greens can then be steamed and eaten with butter and seasonings or combined with other vegetables. Very young sprouts may chopped and used in salads.   Darcy Williamson, who is an old-timer from the high deserts up around Bend, Oregon, wrote a book called "Wild Foods Of The Desert." This book offers some of the wildest gourmet recipes you've ever heard of. But think about this for a moment. Juniper berries, piñon nuts, acorn meal, pickled cactus pads and prickly pear jelly are just a few of the high priced wild desert foods which hold prominent positions on the shelves of the specialty and gourmet shops across the United States.

Let's turn to page 141 of Darcy's book...why, here's a recipe for Tumbleweed Greens that will serve 6.

turn turn

8 Quarts young tumbleweed shoots, chopped

1/2 cup cold water

6 slices bacon

1 egg, lightly beaten

1/4 cup sugar

1/4 cup cider vinegar

1/2 cup water

Put the tumbleweed greens in a kettle and add 1/2 cup of water. Simmer for ten minutes. Fry bacon crisp, crumble and set aside (reserve drippings). Combine egg, sugar, vinegar and 2/4 cup water and pour into drippings in skillet. Heat slowly until slightly thickened. Remove from heat and toss with the cooked greens. Serve garnished with bacon.

Darcy also has recipes for Tumbleweed-Sausage-Lentil stew, Rice & Tumbleweed casserole, Tumbleweed-Pea spring soup, Herbed Tumbleweed, Tumbleweed-Piñon Ring and Tumbleweed Au Gratin. His book is published by Maverick Publications, Bend, Oregon 97701.

Right now, I think I'll go home and whip up a Thistle-noodle casserole!

Cooking with cactus

Prickly pears are perhaps the best known of the cactus plants that are edible. The young pads (3-4" high) are de-spined with a sharp knife, diced and steamed for a dish called "nopalitos." I saute' bacon and chopped onions, add some salt, pepper and a dash of oregano to the drained nopalitos. They will rival the taste of any green bean you've ever eaten!

Every summer I get phone calls telling me that the seed pods of prickly pear cactus (they're called tunas) are ripe. One lady asked: "David, can you please tell me something to do with the tunas besides making jelly? It's too hot to stand by the stove cooking and constantly stirring the juice!" I gave her my recipe for "Never Fail Prickly Pear Jelly." She called back a couple of days later to let me know that her Christmas gift list had been half filled! Here's that recipe:

Gather and wash 4 quarts of red prickly pear fruits. Use tongs to gather these fruits. Twist them off the pad and drop them in a bag or bucket. Wash the fruit in the sink under running water. Drain the fruits and place them in a large kettle along with enough water to barely cover them. Simmer for a half hour. Begin mashing the fruits with a potato masher until all the fruits are crushed. Now, strain the juice through a colander. Throw the seeds and pulp out for the birds to eat! They need a treat too!

Now strain the juice thorough two or three layers of cheesecloth. This takes care of all those little cactus spines. For each quart of juice you cook, you'll need to add 4 cups of sugar and two packages of powdered pectin. Bring this to a boil...slowly. Now remove the juice from the stove and let it cool. Pour the juice into freezer containers or jelly jars. Put them in your freezer a couple of days. When they are removed they're jelly!

If, for some strange reason, your jelly fails to gel, the worst you'll come up with is Cactus Syrup. The pancake lovers in the family will heap much praise upon you for these efforts...you're in a win-win situation! They never had it so good! Try pouring Cactus Syrup over ice cream. This should place you in a win-win-win category, right up there with St. Katrina of the Kitchen! If you have left-over juice, add a little sugar to it and some lemon juice. Now you have a refreshing drink you can serve...call it "Cactus Juice!"

Whenever we have school children tour our botanical garden in Bisbee Junction, we serve them cactus juice. I freeze plastic soda bottles full of the pure juice. When a tour is headed our way, I thaw out a couple of bottles of juice, add 4 or 5 pints of water, a little sugar and a little lemon. Serve chilled. If you want some fizz, try adding a can or lemon-lime soda to the juice. Or, perhaps you'll want to serve "Cactus Juice Popsicles" during the warm months.

I once added sugar to the juice and a package of yeast. I poured all of this into a gallon jug, capped it <u>lightly</u> and let it ferment for a week or so in the cool of my closet. This little drinkie-poo is cleverly called "Cactus Wine." I nearly started a riot when I served this to the Bisbee Rotary Club. They wouldn't let me out of the room until I gave them the recipe!

Some bartenders association should give me an award for mentioning that Cactus Juice and tequila make a good mixed drink!

What's the vitamin content of cactus juice? Well, it supplies you with a pretty large amount of vitamins A and C. It also contains a fair amount of potassium. It is <u>very</u> low in calories.

To arrange a group-tour of Arizona Cactus, complete with "Cactus Juice," call us at (602) 432-7040.

Coyotes both clowns and rebels

One of the toughest and most flexible survivalists found on the desert is the Coyote (Canis latrans). The coyote is the best runner among the canids. They cruise around at about 25 to 30 miles an hour and have been clocked at a little over 40 miles per hour for short distances! Tagged coyotes have been known to travel over 400 miles. That's like travelling from Southeast Arizona to the Grand Canyon, or from Albuquerque, New Mexico to Alpine, Texas!

A Navajo once told me: "The coyote travels far and wide, searching for the heart of the desert. But the desert has no heart, no middle, no beginning and no end. It is like a puzzle without a solution. The coyote knows this, but his free-spirit drives him on, in search of the heart of the desert. Old coyote is a trickster, a rebel against all authority and the breaker of all of our Tribal taboos. He is what the best-behaved person secretly wishes to be. The coyote and his kin represent the freely spontaneous in life, the pure creative spark that defies all rules of behavior. He reminds us that the celebration of life goes on today and he calls us to join him in the frenzy. In an ordered world of objects and labels, he represents the potency of nothingness, of chaos, of freedom...which is a nothingness that always makes something of itself." As I thought of the many coyotes I have seen, he continued..."The coyote and other clowns are sacred to us. A people who have so much to cry about as the American Indians, certainly do need their laughter to survive!"

In the Western areas of North America, many Indian tribes consider the coyote as both an imp and a hero. He is the great culture bearer who can also make mischief beyond belief, turning from clown to the high-priest in the blink of an eye. The Seri Indians, of Northwestern Sonora, Mexico, seek the supernatural powers of the coyote. a person of good eyesight is said to be a member of the "Coyote Clan."

The coyote is one of the few animals that can live with and off of man. There is a large pack of coyotes right in the middle of Griffith park, in central Los Angeles, California. They remain there because nearby residents feed them, or leave their garbage cans where the coyotes can get at them. The coyotes become accustomed to the free handouts and the residents build their 8 and 10 foot fences to keep them out of their yards. The coyote sails over these fences with the greatest of ease.

The old Atomic Energy facility at Los Alamos, New Mexico built a 14-foot high chain link fence around their complex, just to keep the coyotes on their own side of the street. Security guards regularly reported seeing coyotes jump that fence with absolutely no trouble at all.

If there ever was a sound that conjures up images of the West, it's the song of the coyote.

The man that came up with the idea of a pink coyote, made of ceramic or wood, was an imp. Thank you. You've given new life to just about the best symbol the West has.

Now, if we can just revive the old "Roadrunner and Wiley Coyote" cartoons, I'll rejoice until Friday the 33rd...

Scorpions feel the sting of Mexico's inflation

When it's scorpion season in northern Mexico, Durango, Mexico is right in the middle of their monsoon season (they call those summer storms Chubascos). With the additional moisture, the scorpions are seemingly everywhere. Tourists can find the venomous varmints on plates, napkin holders, key-chains and postcards, affixed to shopping bags, whiskey bottles and even embedded in ceramic watermelons!

Oops! I forgot to mention ashtrays...the gift shops and stalls are cluttered with tens-of-thousands of ashtrays that have flattened red scorpions embedded in the glass. Each ashtray is inscribed: "Recuerdos de Durango" (Memories of Durango).

Your "On The Desert" crack reporting team snooped around Durango and found the absolute "King" of scorpion merchandising. He's Joel Moreno, who owns a very large souvenir stall just a couple of blocks from City Hall. Moreno has been shipping his scorpion souvenirs all over Mexico for the past 20 years. But lately, Moreno, like most of his 84 million countrymen, is feeling the sting of inflation!

Joel gingerly cradles a large glass jar containing over 3,000 very dead and very red scorpions, afloat in a brine of alcohol. "Last year these alacranes (scorpions) cost me 15 pesos each. This year, the price has doubled and may even triple before the season is over."

Wait! There's more! Joel says the government is driving up the price of scorpions. He said the government hired his two best scorpion catchers right out from underneath his nose to work for them!

Now, why would the government want to get into such a "growth industry" as scorpion gathering? At first, I thought they might be cashing in on the booming sales of all those ashtrays, key-chains and dinner plates...but Joel says they're rounding up those critters to produce anti-scorpion serum.

Each year during the past 35 years, an average of 430 people die from scorpion stings in Mexico. A few years back, two Durango doctors who live on top of scorpion -infested Calvary Hill, developed a serum to combat the deadly scorpion's sting. Then, the Mexican Government initiated a big campaign to inform the public about the serum and its effectiveness. They have two-man teams of scorpion catchers on their payrolls. They work day and night to catch enough scorpions to produce enough anti-scorpion for all of Mexico.

The serum replaces the popular home cure for scorpion stings...mint tea (yerba buena) brewed with several scorpions.

Moreno says a sort of industrial piracy is going on.

"I go out and hire young men to collect scorpions for my souvenir business. I spend long hours training them," he says. "Then, along comes the government to steal my best workers!"

Scorpions enjoy vivid images in Mexican-Indian mythology. The Nahuatl-speaking peoples from southern Mexico anthropomorphized the scorpion into a very handsome young God, Yappan. Yappan was tempted by Tlazoltectl, the Goddess of Impure Love, only to be discovered by his co-deities. Those other deities didn't take kindly to Yappan's activities and promptly turned him into a scorpion. Yappan was so embarrassed that he hid beneath a stone!

For Durango's city officials, their embarrassment derives more from bad publicity. Durango has a local soccer team sporting the name "Alacranes." The city has tried to rid itself of the dubious honor of being called "The Scorpion Capital of Mexico."

Juan Vargas, who heads up the Durango Tourist Bureau, insists that Acapulco or Cuernavaca should be called the scorpion capital of Mexico. "Scorpions are becoming extinct here...at least in the better hotels." said Vargas.

Displaying a scorpion-distribution map, Durango health administrator Jorge Sanabrea said: "Vargas is right, there is a definite decline in the scorpion population in Durango...why last year, during the height of the scorpion season, which is June, July and August, only three people died from the sting of a scorpion."

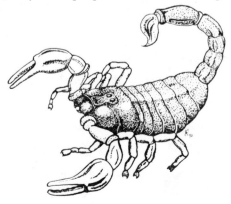

Stranded man lives off cactus four days

A 48-year-old Chandler, Arizona resident survived four days in a remote area of our state by eating prickly pear cactus. He became lost while hiking in Havasupai Canyon, west of Grand Canyon Village.

According to the Associated Press story, the Arizona native walked into the secluded area on the way to Indian Village, a small settlement on the Havasupai Indian Reservation. He had walked to the village to interview for a teaching job. While walking back to the paved road, be strayed from the gravel roadway and walked for hours. He carried along a quart of water for what was originally intended to be a 12-mile hike. When he ran out of water he quickly became dehydrated and lost all sense of direction.

"I didn't ever think I was going to get out, so I ate cactus...thorns and all."

When this article first appeared in print, I received several telephone calls. Most callers asked questions I couldn't answer. What kind of cactus did this man eat? How many? What parts of the plant?

After making several telephone calls, I began to put the pieces of this strange puzzle together.

Several Havasupai Indians found the man about a mile from the oft-traveled and wide main trail. They said his face and hands were red. At first, they thought he was bloodied, but as they came closer to him, they saw that his face was covered with the dried red juice of the seed pods of prickly pear cactus. They said his lips and hands were covered with literally thousands of small reddish-orange spines.

This told me that he was eating the seed pods (tunas) of the red-fruited prickly pear, a variety of Opuntia phaeacantha. The fruits of this cactus are fairly large, about 2 inches long. The juice from those seed pods contain a fair amount of sugar. The seed pods are covered with tiny spines.

All prickly pear cactus are edible; some taste better than others. Generally speaking, the smaller the plant, the more bitter the pads and fruits. The pads of prickly pear cactus are about 95 percent moisture. This moisture is in the form of a mucilaginous sap, much like the gooey slime of okra. This liquid has traditionally been used by Indians of the western deserts much like the peoples of Africa use Aloe Vera. It provides instant relief when applied as a topical ointment for sunburn!

In order to use the plant as a food product, one first has to deal with those spines. They will burn off in seconds when passed over an open flame. Or, you can peel the pads and the fruits. Indians roll the seed pods in sand, using a couple of sticks. Others split the seed pods with a small knife-shaped rock and scrape out the seeds and pulp.

The Indians who found the lost man told me they were looking for stray cattle in the canyon on horseback and didn't know there was a full-scale search underway for the man. They were very surprised to see him in such a remote area.

They gave him a ride back to Indian Village and called the Coconino County Sheriff's Office. None of the rescuers wished to be identified.

"Heck," said one man, "this sort of thing happens at least twice a year, sometimes more often."

Another rhetorically mused..."wonder if he ever heard of a sharp stick...or a sharp rock?"

A law enforcement officer from the area, who also wished to remain anonymous said: "Damn, I hope he doesn't get that school teachers job...we'd probably be looking for him every single weekend!"

Apache Medicine Man's Ten Commandments

Have you ever met a person that you could say is "timeless?" The sort of person whose words and actions would be relevant in the 15th century, the 17th century , or even the 21st century?

Phillip Cassadore was such a man. Phillip was the personification of a "timeless man." After spending a couple of hours talking with Phillip, one could truly walk away with a feeling of enlightenment. People who met Phillip said this feeling usually didn't settle upon them until they had been away from the man for an hour or so. Then, they said that as they thought about their meeting, a feeling of calmness would come over them, and they would seemingly remember every word they heard him speak.

Phillip was an Apache Indian Medicine Man. One of a very few men chosen to help lead his people. We first met in 1980, then again in 1983. Phillip was living in Tucson, trying to persuade the Veterans Administration Hospital doctors that he could assist in the healing of one of their patients ..an old Apache veteran of the Second World War. Phillip said: "The poor man is out of touch with his Mother Earth! Spiritual guidance will help him every bit as much as the medicines they're pumping into him."

The first time I met Phillip, we spent hours talking about the medicinal uses of plants. The next meeting, Phillip spoke to me about the religious beliefs of the Apaches. You see, Phillip believed that his people had their own version of the "Ten Commandments." He said these were unwritten rules (he called them "lessons") to live by.

Phillip died on August 27, 1985, but his words will live forever.

Here are the 10 Lessons that Phillip passed on to younger Apaches. He told me he also wished that the lessons would enrich the lives of all non-Indians.

1. Be humble: do not compete with your friends and relatives.
2. Know your clan...respect all members of your clan.
3. Share with others and teach your children to share.
4. Speak well of others; do not criticize them, their property, or their loved ones.
5. Show reverence for all things...the sun, the land, the water, the mountains, the trees and all creatures upon the earth.
6. Carry with you the white downy eagle feather, yellow pollen and the blue stone, along with the white stone and buckskin. With these, one should pray.
7. Respect your elders. Older people have gained much wisdom throughout their lives. Listen to your grandparents.
8. Be grateful for good fortune. Do not use it to place yourself above others.
9. Remember who you are at all times. You are an Apache Indian! Be proud of your heritage and the history of your people.
10. Walk in beauty. Think only of goodness and stay away from evil.

Water, water everywhere...but

Increased competition for that finite resource...cool, clear and clean water, is causing residents of the arid West to face difficult decisions concerning resource development and water consumption.

California has water cops that bite! One man received a water bill for over $55,000. This included a hefty fine for wasting water. The Lone Star State is gearing up for a water conservation advertising campaign that may rival their great anti-litter effort, titled "Don't Mess With Texas!" Colorado and Utah are "fixin to git busy with the water problem." New Mexico hasn't really brought their horse to the starting gate just because they have lots of mountains in the North, a little river right through the middle of the state and a severe case of Western "Management by Crisis" attitude. Meanwhile, Arizona and Nevada build more golf courses, erect more water fountains and do their best to make their states look like Kentucky. Tucson, Arizona, is one of the few large cities that seems willing to address the problem. Their "Beat The Peak" campaign has worked...but barely.

Here are two interesting charts produced by the Water Education Foundation, of Sacramento, California.

HOW MUCH WATER DO WE USE?

Taking a bath or shower	15-30 Gallons
Washing the dishes	15-60 Gallons
Washing clothes	30 Gallons
Brushing your teeth	1 Gallon
Flushing the toilet (once)	10 Gallons
Daily drinking water	$\frac{1}{2}$ Gallon
Leaking faucet or toilet valve (per day)	6 Gallons
Washing the car	100 Gallons
Watering the lawn and yard	180 Gallons

Please bear in mind that these are averages compiled by the Water Education Foundation and certainly vary from household to household. But I think you'll agree with me...they're shocking! Here are some more...

HOW MUCH WATER DOES IT TAKE TO PRODUCE ONE SERVING OF:

Corn	61 Gallons
Lettuce	6 Gallons
French Fries	6 Gallons
Tomatoes	3 Gallons
Apples	16 Gallons
Cantaloupe	51 Gallons
Cherries	90 Gallons
Oranges	22 Gallons
Watermelon	100 Gallons
Whole Wheat Bread	15 Gallons
Rice	36 Gallons
Almonds	12 Gallons
Margarine	92 Gallons
Beet Sugar	8 Gallons
Milk	65 Gallons
Soft Drink	10 Gallons
Steak	2,607 Gallons
Hamburger	1,303 Gallons
Pork	408 Gallons
Chicken	408 Gallons
Eggs (2)	136 Gallons
Typical Breakfast	209 Gallons
Typical Lunch	1,427 Gallons
Typical Dinner	2,897 Gallons
A Day's Meals (1 person)	4,533 Gallons

Street name crisis!

A crisis of major proportions is rearing its ugly head in the Southwest. Seems those developers of communities and the Planning and Zoning Directors are running out of street names.

City planners claim the developers have used up all the good names they wanted to use years ago. Developers scoff at these charges and hurl counter-charges.

"They're just angry because we came up with Calle De Las Flores Hediondas and they could only think of First Street or Main Street," said the developer of Enchanted New Mesa On The Hill.

"Well, I for one, don't think "Street of the Stinky Flowers" is such a great name," shot back Phineas Frugenmeister, the prestigious Planning and Zoning Director of Patas Chuecas, Arizona. "Besides, out near 436th Place, we already have a street named after some weeds we found there, Mala Yerba Lane, or something like that."

"Not Any more," said the Assistant Planning and Zoning Director. "The courts ruled today that we have to change that name to just plain Mala Lane, because the kids at Jane Mansfield High School (soon to be re-named Cher-Madonna Lyceum) were rolling and smoking every single weed in sight!"

The Entertainment Director at Megafono Village, New Mexico said, "We tried to name a whole bunch of streets after some Indian tribes and the Supreme Court said we gotta pay royalties to the tribes...and now the Chicanos Por La Causa De Todo want retribution for names someone came up with hundreds of years ago"

"You mean to tell me we can't have a Calle Uno or Avenida Dos?" wailed the still-prestigious Phineas.

"No, those kinds of names are alright, according to their guidelines, but we've all really gotta watch out for names like Apache Spiraling Trail and Juan De Las Cabesa De Baca Highway or Beltway," said the winner of happy-hours awards.

Milton Gabfeld, a member of the City Council of Wet Levis, Nevada said: "I feel that those of my race who depend upon bettering their condition in a new community, or who underestimate the importance of cultivating good-will would make friends in every Manly way with the people of all races by whom we are surrounded!"

"What?" someone muttered.

The Mayor of Desperation, California said...

"Milt is right, we must come up with a whole set of brand new names for our avenues, boulevards, expressways, highways, lanes, roads and routes."

"Yeah...and the streets, too," chimed in the Senator from Cold Beer, Texas.

And so, it came to pass that these pillars of their respective communities pooled their shekels and hired "yours truly" to send them some new names.

After giving this serious matter a full thirty seconds of thought, my fingers fairly leapt onto my computer keyboard. I have this program that converts computer languages to latin...or, is it the other way around? Well, PerfectWord (not yet available to just every computer near-whiz) allowed me to come up with the following list for my friends:

Ocotillo Lane - Fouquieria splendens angiportum

Red Bird of Paradise Road - Caesalipinia pulcherrima iter

Saguaro Hill - Carnegia gigantea collis

Barrel Cactus Land - Ferocactus terra

Prickly Pear Way - Aculeatus pirum cursus

Honeysuckle Circle - Justica ghiesbreghtiana orbis

Bottlebrush Avenue - Callistemon citrinus xystus

Poppy Place - Eschscholzia californica locus

Wild Horse Canyon - Ferus equus alveus

Mesquite Hollow - Prosopis glandulosa cavus

Bronze Loquat Street - Eriobotrya deflexa iter

Sugar-bush Heights - Rhus ovatalocus editus

Ash Place - Fraxinus velutina situs

Mint Julep Place - Juniperus chinensis regio

Coral Vine Village - Antigonon leptopus pagus

Nipple-cactus Square - Mammillaria quadratus

Native plants used as natural dyes

A few weeks ago I received a telephone call from a desperate college student living in Santa Fe, New Mexico.

"I'm writing a term paper on Indian uses of native plants as a source of dye and I can't find enough material in any of the libraries here in Santa Fe. Several people suggest I contact you. By the way, do you know you're hard to reach? Your phone has been busy all morning!"

I told the young lady that we just couldn't afford the price of a separate listing in the telephone book and certainly couldn't afford a listing in the Yellow Pages. Maybe someone could donate an answering device to Arizona Cactus, we certainly would use it, but the caller would have to have a rudimentary knowledge of Indian drum signals.

We discussed the Spanish introduction of sheep into the Southwest. I told her how the Navajos once spent a good deal of time raising native cotton or trading for native cotton with the Pueblo tribes, in particular the Zunis.

We also spoke of the carding of wool and then I explained how the Indians wash the wool in soap-suds made from the crushed roots of the Yucca plant. The wool is spun and then colored with plant dyes made from local (or sometimes, not-so-local) plants.

The wool is then dried and washed again in a pot containing a mordant, which permanently fixed the color.

This subject brought to mind a funny story about mordants, which I related to the student:

"I watched an old Indian woman drying some wool by hanging it over a small fire, made of piñon and juniper wood. She spread the wool over a pole and then placed green juniper boughs on the fire. The smoke of the juniper served as the mordant. When I asked if any other substance was used in fixing the color, she began laughing. I can still see her smile and the twinkle in her eyes as she asked her husband to bring her a pot which reeked of urine. I respectfully declined her request to add to the pot!

Here's a list of some dye sources that I passed on to this determined scholar:

Black: Sunflower seeds plus piñon gum, or Sumac leaves mixed with yellow ocher.

Blue: Blue Hopi bean, Native Indigo, Antelope brush or Bur-sage.

Purple: Wild larkspur flowers or Native purple corn kernels.

Red: Wild plum roots

Pink: Prickly pear cactus fruits, Pincushion cactus fruits, Coxcomb, Indian tea or Pucoon root

Yellow: Rabbitbrush flowers, Salt bush, Linoncillo, Snakeweed or Rubber plant

Brown: Canaigre dock

Orange: Mountain mahogany

Tan: Alder bark, Mormon tea, Mesquite roots or inner bark, Juniper twigs or Jatropha roots

Green: Russian thistle, Mountain ball sage or Lupine flowers.

This is by no means a complete list of the plants used as sources of dye by the Indian tribes of the Southwest.

Many tribes traded for dye sources...travelling many hundreds of miles to accomplish these trades. With the appearance of synthetic dyes in the late 1850's, the use of vegetal dyes declined with many of the Indian tribes.

The exceptions to this were the traditionalists among blanket and basket weavers.

Fortunately, there is a renewed interest among many weavers and crafts-people in the use of natural dyes. Our native plants offer up an unending variety of subtle shades of dye. If you collect any of these plants, or plant parts...be nice to the earth and do not denude any plant from any area!

Ocotillo

The Ocotillo (pronounced oh-ko-**tee**-yo) is one of the desert plants which gives character to the arid lands of the Southwestern United States and the Mexican states of Chihuahua, Sonora, Baja California, Coahuila, Nuevo Leon, Durango, Zacatecas and San Luis Potosi. Actually, (or, as my friend Bucky used to say..."to tell the truth...") there are 11 species of this plant, with perhaps the most unusual being the "Boojum Tree."

I, for one, have a hard time with the proper placement of the plant within the Fouquieriaceae family. All of its distant relatives are bushes and in many cases, trees. The botanical community might well do itself a favor and move it over to the Polemoniaceae family.

Within the United States, the plant is perhaps the most widespread of the "high profile" plants. It begins in the lower Rio Grande Valley of Texas, then is spotted across the vast Edwards Plateau region. It is also found in the Trans-Pecos portion of the Lone Star State. In New Mexico, it is almost exclusively found in the Southern part of the state. It is widespread in Arizona, found almost state-wide below 5,000 feet in elevation. In California, it is found in the extreme Southwestern Mojave desert and on the Colorado desert. I have also seen small scattered colonies of Ocotillo in Southern Nevada.

The first time I saw the plant, I can remember thinking: "Why, it looks like a bundle of fishing rods sticking out of the ground." Quite a few years later, I found out, the hard way, that a stalk of the plant really can't be used for a fishing rod. Why? Well...It breaks too easily.

There are a number of common names for the plant, among them: Coach whip, Vine-cactus and Jacob's staff. Of these names, perhaps the worst is Vine-cactus...for it certainly isn't a vine and is **not** a cactus.

During most of the year, the plant looks very much like a bunch of old dead sticks, towering sometimes 30 feet above the desert floor. But during the summer months, when the plant receives rain, a tight cluster of red flowers appears at the tip of each branch, Soon, the branches are covered with small green leaves. These leaves wither and die when the plant runs out of moisture stored inside just for this reproduction process. Give the plant some water and it will repeat this entire process. I've seen this happen as many as seven times in one year!

One of the first written accounts of Ocotillo was made by Frederick Wislizenus. He was perhaps, the most "unbotanical collector" who ever entered the field. But, when it was all said and done, this "booted wagoneer" managed to describe a multitude of plants, then unknown to mankind. He's the one who "crawled" over the old Santa Fe Trail...all of it. One night, while camped near a rare desert stream down in Chihuahua, Mexico, he wrote these words about the Ocotillo:

"April 27, 1847. Marched 20 miles today. In the chaparral I met with different species of cacti in blossom: a small odd tree with green thorns (Koeberlinia) and also the purple-flowered Ocotillo. I had seen this plant in the Jornada del Muerto, above El Paso, but not in bloom. As it is one of the most common and obnoxious plants in the chaparrals, I will give its description. It grows in long branchless stalks, but a dozen of them standing together, covered all over with thorns, with few and quite small leaves and at the upper end of the stalk a cluster of purple flowers. They grow generally from 10 to 20 feet high: sometimes I have seen them at a height of 30 feet. The Mexicans use them sometimes for hedges." *

Full-sized stems of Ocotillo may be placed in suggestively moist soil and they will re-root themselves. Have patience, because this process can take up to two years. Some say: "Don't forget to hold your teeth just right while yer a'waitin!"

* From Wislizenus' "Tour of Northern Mexico." Fascinating reading, available from Rio Grande Press, Glorieta, New Mexico 87535

The plant is widely used for fencing and for the support of thatched roofs of ramadas. The flowers of the plant are edible, albeit somewhat bitter.

The Apache Indians of Southeast Arizona used to travel regularly to the Rio Grande Valley of New Mexico. Their final destination was a place called Hot Springs (today known as Truth or Consequences). This was one long hike! Many of the Indians I talked to told me stories similar to this one:

"We gathered the flowers of the Ocotillo and carried them along with us on our journey. When we could come upon a pool of fresh water, we would dam it and separate it from the stream. Then, we would crush the flowers of the "Red One" and throw them into the water. We would stir this with a stick, then allow the water to settle. There, we bathed our hot and tired feet...this greatly relieved our fatigue!"

Artwork by Mimi Kamp

Excerpts from my field journal

Intensely hot days are no rarity to the deserts of Coahuila, Mexico. Our field work has brought us to this "hot spot" on the face of the earth in search of a different variety of Bishop's Cap Cactus" (Astrophytum myriostigma). My field notes for July 27, 1959 tell the story...

"It's nearly 8:00 in the morning and already the glistening sun produces a heavy heat which pushes down upon Nicho and I.

Far over toward the Southwest, I can dimly see the outline of a mountain chain. Another fifty miles of bouncing along this poor excuse for a dirt road should put us very close to our destination. The dust is as fine as face powder. Nicho and I wear bananas soaked with water over our faces. I chuckle at the thought of what we must look like...a couple of modern day <u>bandidos</u>, no doubt! The valley ahead of us is covered with a dim, yellow haze. The plants around us have been twisted and crippled by the heat. Slowly...maybe we're doing 10 miles an hour...we work our way down to the floor of the valley.

We've been on the road for at least three hours and barely managed to make 5 miles! Nicho rattles off words like <u>dull</u> and <u>monotonous</u>. My spirits have become brittle with the heat. I feel I am incapable of expression. I am mildly angered by Nicho's description of the vista before us. You see, I'm young...and...how I love it all! How ardently I love it...this unending, wild, unlimited desert! Out here is where man should live...where beauty and genuineness are the natural law!

We clatter down onto the floor of the valley and begin to pick up speed. 15...20 miles an hour. Nicho shifts to second gear. I think to myself..."that's the first time we've used second gear since we started out this morning!" I hang my head out of the window of the Jeep to catch a breath of fresh air. but the air dries out my bandanna. I remove it and wet it down, holding my breath until I can again fasten it over my mouth and nose. Ahead, glimmering heat-waves sweep along, seemingly destroying all life with a flow that singes the plants. I twist in the seat and look behind us. There's nothing to see but a big cloud of dust...rising 20, no, make that 30 feet into the sky, blocking my view of the mountain we've just descended.

Nicho wants me to look at the map again. The <u>map</u> is a piece of cardboard on which Don Jose drew directions to a water hole named "La Noria" (The deep well). Don Jose said it was the only water we would find for at least a hundred kilometers in any direction! I study the map and remember the words of Don Jose: "When you come down off the big mountain, it's only about 60 kilometers across the valley to La Noria. About 20 kilometers before you get to the mountains on the far (south) side of the valley, there's an old trail that leads off to the west, towards Las Delicias. Even in your Jeep, you cannot travel this road! It is Coahuila's answer to the Sahara!"

Off to the right, about a mile ahead, is a road heading west. I scan the horizon from the top of a rise we've just come upon. I imagine I've just seen some smoke far off in the distance. "Probably breakfast at Delicias," Nicho quips.

I watch the odometer roll on as we head into a group of low hills. We're up off the valley floor a little now. We slow to 5 miles an hour and pick our way around the limestone boulders strewn about the roadway by some giant who didn't want visitors at his water-hole.

The sun is at high noon, we have rounded the mountain and there before us, in the brightly glowing sun, is an oasis! "La Noria" is visible just below us. It never looked so good!...to anyone! A narrow path leads down to the crystal clear water. Nicho and I clamber down the hillside to the edge of the water and splash ourselves with the cool, wet and wonderful water! A narrow arroyo winds its way beyond the water-hole. This thoughtful little arroyo has given life to 8 Mesquite trees, with their shade-giving branches. Beyond the mesquites, up on the side of the mountain, my eye catches a glimpse of something shining...seemingly white. The cactus plants we came to see! There they are! I look up the side of the mountain and as far as I can see...probably 200 yards to the top...the hillside is covered with the rare plants. Thousands of them! What a gorgeous display of nature!

A boy's desert treasure hunt...

It was right after praying class that some of the bigger boys in our glass jumped me. I'll never forget it. I was whizzing up the stairs at Mach 5, on my way to my special class in "speed latin." These guys sat in the back of the last class, right by the door. As the rest of the class formed their little faces for the "Amen," (the kind with the long AAAAAAAAaaaaaaAAAAAAAaaaaa...men!) these guys just said "men" and split!

With that three-second advantage, they were all standing around up on the first stair landing, waiting for "Yours Truly." I came to a screeching halt because Julio's hand was tangled up in my shirt, just about collar-high.

Now, Julio was a 6'2" fourteen-year-old who was being petitioned out of the 5th grade. But there was a big lobby of athletic supporters who wanted him to stick around for an unprecedented <u>third</u> undefeated season in our school league.

Julio directed my body to a corner while his little playmates removed my shoes and my belt, preventing me from running away or doing a venial sin by telling them I had a "black belt."

"Tell us where you and Dr. Oso are going this weekend." Julio hissed. Billy agreed by hissing twice.

"If it's Farmington, I want a ride as far as Shiprock," said Johnny.

"Are you guys going to Grants? I get to ride up front with you and Dr. Oso...and if you don't agree right this minute, I'll "Indian-burn" your wrists until they bleed." growled Julio.

This last threat was the kind one takes seriously...'cause Julio was warming up his hands for the "Pachey Way Of Hurting The Enemy" ceremony. My left wrist already hurt something fierce and Julio wasn't even warmed up!

I quickly told these three upstanding citizens everything they wanted to know...and more!

These guys were classmates whose families lived out on the Indian reservations around Gallup. They sent their children in to town for schooling. Some of the children lived in boarding-houses during the week and wanted to get a chance to visit their homes, even if it was just for a few hours while Dr. Castetter (we called him Dr. oso) talked to the older Indians of their tribe. I was Dr. Oso's note-taker. Scribble like mad on a 5-cent "Big Chief" tablet while the elders told Dr. Castetter how they used the native plants for food, clothing and medicine. I would later transcribe these notes into a readable form of English and forward them to Dr. Castetter's office at the University of New Mexico in Albuquerque. I think it was Sister Mary (most of us called her Sister Mary Elephant, because she was large) who got me the job. I thanked her then and again this morning at daybreak, as I wrote this.

"We're going to Fence Lake!"

That was all I could say before passing out after a full five-tenths of a second of having my wrist skin being separated from my body.

"Why didn't you say so earlier?" asked Johnny.

"You could have died within the next instant," Billy continued, "however, we'll forget all about this if you and Dr. Oso pick us up at six on Saturday morning."

I instantly agreed and they were kind enough to allow me to tie my shoes and then they gave me back my much coveted black belt.

Saturday morning found the four of us and Dr. Oso, driving the wagon ruts out to Zuni. The May spring morning was clear and cold as we chugged our way in and out of the piñon forest west of Gallup.

"Boys, today I want to show you where there's a treasure hidden in the ground." said Dr. Oso.

At Zuni we turned east, towards Ramah. Southeast for another 8 miles and there was Inscription Rock, looming almost above us. As Dr. Oso maneuvered the old University of New Mexico Chevy car up and down the hills, he kept up a steady lecture about the history of Inscription Rock. Julio asked: "Is Roy Rogers' name on the wall?"

Dr. Oso turned abruptly to the southwest and we followed an old wagon trail down toward the "malpais," a broken zig-zag string of black volcanic lava rock dotting the landscape. This was the "old" wagon trail to Zuni...the one that went right through the Ramah-Navajo Indian Reservation.

Now, all of us thought Dr. Oso was going to have us collect some plants for him. Before visiting Indians who were willing to share information with him, Dr. Oso always collected the plants he would be asking about. "Correct identification of plants is imperative," he always said.

The car slowed and Dr. Oso looked up towards a black ridge of volcanic rock.

"Boys...see those caves up there? Let's go have a look," said Dr. Oso.

The five of us climbed the fifty feet or so to the caves. They were small...with two-foot wide openings, all blocked by large hunks of volcanic rock. Dr. Oso helped us move one of the rocks and Julio was the first to scramble into the cave, which was about 5-feet deep. Dr. Oso's flashlight lit up the back of the cave, where the light beam fell upon the **most beautiful** vase I had ever seen! The four of us could only gasp...! Dr. Oso's words were: "Oh My!"

The vase was about 18 inches high. Next to the vase was an old pair of sandals, made of Yucca Fiber. The minute Dr. Oso's eyes fell upon those sandals, he said: "let's go boys!"

We backed out of the cave and Dr. Oso said: "Let's get this rock back in place. David, you and Billy go find some other rocks so we can block this entrance. This is a sacred spot that we must not disturb anymore than we already have."

Dr. Oso's long gone...so is Julio. Alcohol fried his brain. But today I know that three people still remember the valuable lesson we learned from Dr. Oso on that fine May morning. We still have the treasure!

55

-epilogue-

"Don Carlos" speaks to us about water

Seems like it was just yesterday, but it was 36 years ago, while on a field trip to northern Coahuila, Mexico, I picked up an entire family hitch-hiking from Boquillas del Carmen to the area around Cuatro Cienegas. Since both areas are considered "plant heaven" to botanists, it was really no big surprise to learn that I had just picked up five of Northern Mexico's most noted, self-taught, botanists. They were "curanderos" who knew the medicinal uses of every plant, living or dead, of the Chihuahuan desert!

Seems they had been attending a meeting of their peers up around Sanderson, Texas. They were on their way south to collect plants for their "Mail-order" herb business.

Our seven-hour drive was filled with conversation about the plants and animals of the desert we were crossing. The wisest words were those of the old man, "Don Carlos." This 92 year-old man lectured us on the abilities of plants and animals to survive in such a harsh environment. Almost impolitely, I asked Don Carlos to tell me of the most important thing(s) that he had learned during all of his years travelling on the deserts.

He replied: "David, the three most important things you can ever learn about the desert are:

1. HOW TO GET (FIND) MOISTURE
2. HOW TO KEEP (STORE) MOISTURE
3. HOW TO USE MOISTURE WISELY

At that time, those words just didn't sink in. Sure, I remembered the "dust bowl" years somewhat, but they were behind us. I lived in the Rio Grande Valley in

Central New Mexico, where there was plenty of water. The United States was building dams to store that water. There were dams and lakes on the drawing boards to satisfy the water needs of all desert dwellers, in the U.S. and Mexico!

It was not until some ten years later that I began to "hear" those words of Don Carlos. I began to realize that the great lands of the West were going to come up short of water in future years...an assessment of values was in order.

Was it really O.K. for us to use the same farming techniques that were commonly practiced in the Eastern and Mid-western parts of the United States? Wasn't there a fundamental difference in climate to contend with? If there is a huge underground cavern of water straddling the United States-Mexican border...whose water is it? Who dictates the use of that water? Could we ever expect to be required to share that water with our neighbors? When will Juarez' population top 6 million? Is there such a thing as a drinking straw for 7 million?

It was about 1965 that I first heard of a plan to move water from the Great Lakes down across the Midwest and into the Western United States. Then I learned of another plan to get water to the parched West. Water would be diverted from the Colombia and Snake Rivers!

Both plans have been dismissed as too grandiose and too inflammatory.

With "El Niño" and the "Greenhouse Effect" upon us, perhaps those plans will be drug out, dusted off and looked at once more...not to water the crops...but to save the people!

One thing's for sure, the problem is upon us. And it certainly isn't going to go away!

Which Western state will lead the way in establishing ground rules for the transfer of water from the "haves" to the "have nots?" Arizona took a bold step ten years ago, but then quietly settled down to sleep on the matter. Will New Mexico take the lead? Texas? California will probably lead the nation in the number of radical new water conservation laws. What about Colorado, Utah and Nevada?

Just what is the status of the desalinization of sea water? We've long had the ability to supply an Aircraft Carrier with fresh water on a daily basis...why not an entire city? It's just about time we saddled up old Paint and rode out to meet this challenge folks. In fact, it's past time! Our water is our future!

"On The Desert" will keep you abreast of the latest developments concerning water and the desert Southwest.

For instance...

* I have a copy of a Water Treaty between Mexico and the United States lying on my desk.
* There's a plan on the drawing boards to turn Colorado River water into steam, then into power, utilizing solar power at the front end.
* Politicians are privately and seriously questioning the wisdom of supporting farming, ranching and mining in the West.
* Will growth limits be enacted throughout the West?
* You seed my cloud...I'll seed yours...fact or fiction?
* Will the Indians have the last laugh?
* Will Phineas "discover" solar power in Patas Chuecas?
* "Do The Right Thing" -vs- "Keep On Scammin' On"
* Will Joseph Eppele send more line drawings?

"On The Desert" is read in 22 Western cities and towns. By this time next year, I hope it's read in 222 cities and towns. Self-syndication isn't glamorous, doesn't make one rich and surely is a lot of work! But I love it...and I love you, dear reader. You're part of what makes this West still as awe-inspiring as it ever was. Your cards, letters and phone calls all push me forward...to look...to listen...to ask...to drive....and then report back to you. What's going on? Who's minding the store? Have you ever seen a Sun Dog? Is Texas really that big? Have you paid your <u>rain tax?</u>

If your local paper doesn't carry "On The Desert" hound the Editor, Publisher and/or owner until they are completely fed-up with you! Then give him my phone number: 1-602-432-7040. Or my address:

David L. Eppele
Arizona Cactus
8 Mulberry Lane
Bisbee, Arizona 85603

You've just finished reading "On The Desert" Vol. 1. Thank you...so very much. DLE